I0202372

CALLED OUT!

Kingdom Living for Missional Teens

Jenny Rae Armstrong and Aaron Armstrong

Christians for Biblical Equality
cbeinternational.org

Called Out! Kingdom Living for Missional Teens

© 2013 by Jenny Rae Armstrong and Aaron Armstrong

Published by Christians for Biblical Equality
122 W Franklin Ave, Suite 218
Minneapolis, MN 55404
cbeinternational.org

All rights reserved. No part of this publication may be reproduced, stored in a retrieval system, or transmitted in any form or by any means—for example, electronic, photocopy, recording—without the prior written permission of the publisher. The only exception is brief quotation in printed reviews.

All references to the NIV are to the 2010 revision: THE HOLY BIBLE, NEW INTERNATIONAL VERSION®, NIV® Copyright © 1973, 1978, 1984, 2010 by Biblica, Inc.™ Used by permission. All rights reserved worldwide.

Design: Elizabeth Beyer

ISBN-13: 978-1-939971-01-2

Printed in the United States of America

CONTENTS

Introduction

What is the goal of this curriculum?

God didn't create people to just lounge around in a garden, napping in the sun and popping grapes. We were made to be active agents in creation, God's ambassadors to the world! This theologically-rich curriculum traces the missional meta-narrative woven throughout scripture, from creation and the call of Abraham, to Christ's revolutionary kingdom and the Spirit-empowered church. Students will be equipped with practical ideas on how to live purposefully as part of the body of Christ, and challenged to go "all in," developing their gifts and pursuing God's calling on their life.

Each session includes (feel free to use the sections in any order):

- A short video.

- A Bible reading.

- A narrative overview of the Bible reading, focusing on the session's theme.

- Discussion questions to facilitate conversation—no "yes or no" questions or fluffy fill-in-the-blanks.

- A hands-on group activity for tangible learning.

Curriculum Outline

Session 1: Created "On Purpose"
Overview: People weren't created to just lounge around in a garden,

napping in the sun and popping grapes! As God's image-bearers, we are made to be active agents in creation, pouring everything God created us to be back into God's purposes for the world. Emphasis is on purposeful stewardship of our gifts, abilities, and lives.

The chapter will explore what it might mean to bear God's image and "be fruitful," including women's creation as *ezer kenegdo*. *Ezer kenegdo*, or "helper suitable," does not mean that women are to be men's assistants, or imply subjugation. In English, 'strong ally' would be a better description. Men and women are to work alongside each other, with equal authority and responsibility, to work out God's purposes in the world he entrusted to our care.

Session 2: The Curse and the Counterstrike: Stomping on Snakes
Overview: When humanity rebelled against God, all of creation was thrown into chaos. But God refused to leave us in our mess. He unveiled his rescue plan, a plan that he invited (and still invites) his image-bearers to participate in. But it wasn't going to be easy, for anyone. The emphasis of this chapter is on coping with conflict.

This lesson will explain that as followers of Christ, we are NOT called to live in the curse — we're called to live in the redemption! We'll always have to face challenges in this world, but we're called to stand against them, not propagate them.

Session 3: The People of the Promise: Then and Now
Overview: God decided to call a special people to himself, and make them a blessing to all people. They would not only demonstrate what it looks like to live in relationship with God, but carry the promise of the Messiah in their very being. The emphasis is on faith, obedience, and action.

The main purpose of this lesson is to give examples of women and men who stepped forward in faith and obedience even (and especially!) when it broke their society's mold. The big activity for this lesson will involve looking at a quick synopsis of the lives of several Old Testament characters, explaining how their actions were risky or unconventional, and asking the students to choose which one they have the most in common with, and why. For instance, Esther was a woman who always seemed to accept society's view of her value (which was based on her beauty and submissiveness), and went along with everyone else's plans for her life, until a huge crisis forced her into action, drawing out the courage, tenacity, intelligence, and leadership ability that she probably never knew she had.

Session 4: The Unconventional King(dom)

Overview: Abraham's descendants had been waiting for the messiah for 2,000 years, but when he showed up, he wasn't what they expected. This chapter will look at the unconventional kingdom of God, as taught by Jesus.

This lesson will include Jesus' egalitarian treatment of women and the ways he refused to let them be marginalized. It will talk about how Jesus ignored the social norms that limited women, and scolded his disciples when they tried to enforce them. One example is the fact that while there were twelve men who accompanied him on his journeys, there were "the women" who accompanied him as well—Joanna, Suzanna, Mary Magdelene, etc. Another is the example of Mary of Bethany, who sat at Jesus feet to hear him teach. The lesson will explain why Martha was REALLY upset about Mary "sitting at Jesus' feet" (because she was putting herself in the role of a disciple, which was forbidden to women). Even Jesus' conception was unconventional—he was born to a teenage girl who accepted God's calling on her life (without consulting her father or fiancé!). And of course, it was a woman who was the first person to bear witness to the resurrected Jesus.

Session 5: Wind and Fire: An Unstoppable Combination

Overview: The disciples gathered in the upper room were already saved. They were followers of Jesus who had been forgiven of their sins.

But when the Holy Spirit was poured out on them at Pentecost, they were empowered for ministry in a special way. The emphasis is on the empowerment of God's people by the Holy Spirit and the importance of "remaining in Christ" to bear fruit.

This session will talk about the outpouring of the Holy Spirit, empowering all God's people for ministry in a special way, and the way it broke down gender, ethnic, and socio-economic boundaries.

Session 6: Being the Body: Rocking your Role and Living in Love
Overview: We're all one in Christ, but that doesn't mean we're all the same. We've all been given gifts, but they're not just for us — they're to benefit the whole body of Christ.

This session will cover why it's so important to discover and develop your spiritual gifts, and encourage others to do the same. But a big part of this session will be about not quenching the work of the Spirit in someone else's life, encouraging them instead of limiting them. This is SO crucial! Emphasis is on operating in unity, spurring one another on toward love and good deeds, and doing everything in a spirit of love.

SESSION 1

— 1 —

Created "On Purpose"

Optional Bible Reading:

Genesis 1

Primary Texts:

So God created mankind in his own image, in the image of God he created them; male and female he created them. God blessed them and said to them, "Be fruitful and increase in number; fill the earth and subdue it. Rule over the fish in the sea and the birds in the sky and over every living creature that moves on the ground" (Genesis 1:27-28).

For we are God's handiwork, created in Christ Jesus to do good works, which God prepared in advance for us to do (Ephesians 2:10).

Created "On Purpose"

Imagine the world as the first man and woman must have experienced it. Lush trees loaded down with low-hanging fruit, silver fish darting in streams of diamond-clear water, the cool creation breeze brushing the prickling heat of the sun off your skin.

God was thrilled with his creation, and especially pleased with the human beings he created to look after the earth on his behalf. They were God's pride and joy, made in his image—creative, relational beings who would delight in discovering and developing all the good things the world had to offer, just as God had delighted in creating it. In Genesis 1:28, God has a conversation with the man and the woman, giving them instructions like a proud parent unleashing their kids on the adventure of a lifetime.

> Be fruitful and increase in number; fill the earth and subdue it. Rule over the fish in the sea and the birds in the sky and over every living creature that moves on the ground.

Read the first sentence of God's instructions to the man and the woman again. "Be fruitful and increase in number; fill the earth and subdue it." Most of the time when people read this verse, they think God was just telling Adam and Eve to have kids and populate the Earth. But there's more to it than that. This is humanity's mission statement, echoed in the Great Commission Jesus gave his followers—to go into all the world and make disciples of all nations (Mark 16:15, Matthew 28:19). Each and every one of us is called to be fruitful in using our unique God-given gifts to enlarge God's kingdom, to bring honor to God's name and justice to our world, and to increase the number of disciples of Jesus who will reflect God's image to the world as it is "in heaven."

Talk About It

- Genesis 1:27 says that people are created "in the image of God." What do you think that means?

- What do you think God means when he tells the humans to rule over creation?

- We think about Adam and Eve being banished from the Garden of Eden as punishment (which it was), but did you notice that God had already told them to "fill the earth"? What do you think God wanted them to do outside the Garden?

- Who is God telling to rule over creation? The male? The female? Or both of them together? Do you think this is significant?

Allies and Ezers

> The Lord God said, "It is not good for the man to be alone. I will make a helper suitable for him" (Genesis 2:18).

Genesis 1 gives us the big picture of creation, from the dazzling burst of light that exploded upon the cosmos at God's command, to the quieter, but no less magnificent, creation of humankind. In Genesis 1, the male and female are given the exact same task: to use their image-of-God intellect and creativity to rule and subdue creation on God's behalf, working together to make God's vision for the world a reality.

Genesis 2 zooms in on the creation of Adam and Eve, and for many people, this is where things get confusing. Just as a misunderstanding about what it means to subdue the earth has done a lot of damage to the environment, a misunderstanding about what God created women to do and be has done a lot of damage to human relationships.

In Genesis 2, God creates Adam first, then creates Eve as his "helper." Some people think this means women are supposed to be men's assistants — that it was Adam's job to rule and subdue, and Eve was there to help him out, to keep him company and manage the details of domestic life, freeing Adam up for bigger, better things.

But this not only contradicts what the Bible says in Genesis 1, it isn't even an accurate description of what Genesis 2 means!

In Hebrew, the word that is translated as "helper" is *ezer*. An *ezer* is not a servant, secretary, or junior assistant—in fact, the word *ezer* has military overtones, and usually refers to Israel's military allies, or to God himself. An *ezer* is not weaker than or subservient to the person they are "helping"—if they were, they wouldn't be much help at all!

In English, the word "ally" might be a better description. It is not good for the man to be alone. I will make an ally for him. Allies are two distinct entities who work together to accomplish a common goal—in this case, caring for and building up the world God created. God gave every human being, male and female, the same job description in Genesis 1:28. And God expects everyone to bring each and every ounce of the talent, intellect, and creativity he has blessed us with to the task of being fruitful with our God-given gifts and calling, carrying out God's purposes in the world.

Talk About It

- Does the meaning of *ezer* surprise you? Does it challenge your understanding of how God wants men and women to relate to each other, or confirm what you have believed all along?

- Think about someone who has been an *ezer* to you—a friend, a relative, a coach, a teacher. How has having them in your corner impacted your life?

A Unique Reflection of God's Character

For we are God's handiwork, created in Christ Jesus to do good works, which God prepared in advance for us to do (Ephesians 2:10).

Think about this. Before the first fingers of light stretched out across the cosmos, before the first fat drops of water collected in Earth's primordial seas, before the first fine particles of matter were shaped into a human form, God was thinking about you—delighting in the amazing person he would create you to be, grieving over your hurts, disappointments and failures, and weaving together a providential purpose for your life. Absolutely unique, you were put here on purpose to reflect the image of God in a way that only you can.

God gave us all the same job description, but that doesn't mean we all fulfill it in the same way! 1 Corinthians 12:4-6 explains,

> There are different kinds of gifts, but the same Spirit distributes them. There are different kinds of service, but the same Lord. There are different kinds of working, but in all of them and in everyone it is the same God at work.

Make no mistake. God created you, and every other person in this room, for a reason. He put you here, in this time and place, for a purpose. And even when life is hard, when horrible things happen that are contrary to God's will, God's plans and purposes for you are good.

And those purposes aren't just the ones we think of as religious or spiritual. From the very beginning, God intended for men and women, boys and girls, to bring their full strength, creativity, intelligence, and determination to building the world God envisioned. There were cities to be constructed, mountains to be climbed, seas to be conquered, continents to be explored. There were songs to be written, masterpieces to be painted, technology to be invented, a whole world of wonders to be discovered. Human beings' desire to build, to create, to use the raw materials God provided to come up with something new, is one of the unique ways that we reflect our endlessly creative creator God.

Talk About It

- What are some great human "creations" that have had a big impact on your life? A favorite book or movie? Medicine that keeps a loved one healthy? The phone that lets you chat with your grandma who lives in another state? Do you think God was pleased with the work people did to create them?

- Do you have any ideas about why God put you in this time and place? Talk about it!

Activity: How I see God's Image In You

Divide up into groups of 5-10, and sit in a circle. (The groups should be as large as time allows.) Focusing on one person at a time, go around the circle, and have everyone say one thing that they appreciate about that person. How they stood up for a kid who was being picked on at school, how good they are at troubleshooting technological problems, how they listen to everyone without judging. The person being complimented is not allowed to say anything but "thank you." When everyone has said something good about that person, move on to the next person in the circle.

Explain to the students that the compliments must be sincere—no teasing or underhanded insults. If a student doesn't know the person being complimented, or honestly has nothing to say, have them say "pass," and move on to the next person. (Try to put the students in groups where this will be minimized.)

SESSION 2

— 2 —

Stomping on Serpents: the Kingdom Strikes Back!

Optional Bible Reading

Genesis 3

Primary Texts

When the woman saw that the fruit of the tree was good for food and pleasing to the eye, and also desirable for gaining wisdom, she took some and ate it. She also gave some to her husband, who was with her, and he ate it. Then the eyes of both of them were opened, and they realized they were naked; so they sewed fig leaves together and made coverings for themselves (Genesis 3:6-7).

Liar, Liar

What were they thinking?!

There Adam and Eve were in the Garden of Eden, with everything they needed to live happily ever after. (The Bible could have been a much shorter book!) If they were hungry, they could choose from the delicious array of fruits weighing down the tree branches. If they were lonely, they could wander over to the other for a chat, no drama or insecurity involved. There was no shortage of interesting, fulfilling work to be done, and the animals must have provided great entertainment, no YouTube app necessary!

Best of all, Adam and Eve got to walk with God in the cool of the evening, talking, learning, and enjoying God's company. Imagine being able to bring all your thoughts, questions, and concerns to God, and getting an immediate answer!

But for some reason, they weren't satisfied.

Genesis 3 records the greatest tragedy in human history, instigated by a cunning serpent with an evil agenda. (Never trust a talking snake!) Genesis 3:1-3 says,

> Now the serpent was more crafty than any of the wild animals the Lord God had made. He said to the woman, "Did God really say, 'you must not eat from any tree in the garden'?" (Genesis 3:1).

Do you notice how the serpent is twisting the truth, asking if God said they can't eat ANY of the fruit in the garden? It's a cleverly calculated move that makes God sound like the bad guy, like a miserable miser who isn't looking out for Eve and Adam's best interests.

Instead of telling the creeper to get lost, Eve decides to set the serpent straight.

> The woman said to the serpent, "We may eat fruit from the trees in the garden, but God did say, 'You must not eat fruit from the tree that is in the middle of the garden, and you must not touch it, or you will die'" (Genesis 3:1).

Well, actually, God didn't say that bit about not touching the fruit—at least it's not recorded in scripture. Avoiding the fruit is certainly a good idea, but Eve is adding her own rules to God's (you—the leader—may need to be prepared to address why Eve added to the rules of Eden).

"You will not certainly die," the serpent said to the woman. "For God knows that when you eat from it your eyes will be opened, and you will be like God, knowing good and evil" (Genesis 3:4-5).

At this point, Eve and Adam have a choice to make. Are they going to believe the serpent, or believe God? Are they going to trust that God is looking out for their best interests, or doubt God's love, and decide that they could do a better job looking after themselves? Are they going to do the hard work of reflecting God's image by walking closely with and learning from God, or are they going to try to be LIKE God without being WITH God?

Tragically, Eve and Adam made the wrong choice. They bought into the lie, bit into the fruit, and nothing was ever the same again.

Talk About It

- Why do you think the serpent asked if Adam and Eve weren't allowed to eat any of the fruit in the Garden? Can you think of other situations where someone has twisted the truth, or told a half-truth, to make a lie more believable? Explain.

- Eve told the serpent that she and Adam weren't allowed to even touch the fruit, though God had only told them not to eat it. Put yourself in Eve's place for a minute—what do you think Eve thought when she touched the fruit, and nothing bad happened? Has a similar thing ever happened to you?

- What do you think Eve and Adam should have done when they began to doubt whether God had told them the truth about the fruit?

Truth and Consequences

> Then the man and his wife heard the sound of the Lord God as he was walking in the garden in the cool of the day, and they hid from the Lord God among the trees of the garden. But the Lord God called to the man, "Where are you?" (Genesis 3:8-9).

When Adam and Eve rebelled against God, all of creation was thrown into chaos. Like children who had just broken an invaluable treasure, they sensed it and hid, until God called them out of hiding.

> ...Who told you that you were naked? Have you eaten from the tree that I commanded you not to eat from?...What is this that you have done? (Genesis 3:11,13)

You can almost hear God's anguish over Adam and Eve's lost innocence. God knows the consequences that are coming — consequences that Adam and Eve are only beginning to comprehend.

"It was this woman you put here with me," Adam said, shifting the blame to Eve — and to God.

"The serpent deceived me, and I ate," said Eve, shirking responsibility for her decision.

The serpent remained silent and unrepentant.

After they were done making excuses, God explained the consequences their actions would bring about, the curse that sin unleashed on the world.

Their relationship with God was broken, marred by sin and shame.

Their relationship with one another was broken. Instead of enjoying that close, equal relationship God created them to have, the man would try to rule over the woman, and she, in her desire to be loved, would let him.

The earth was broken. It would become difficult to cultivate, forcing them to labor hard just to survive.

Their bodies were broken. The woman would suffer greatly trying to bring new life into the world, and in the end, everyone would die.

Satan had dealt a devastating blow. But God refused to leave his good creation in this horrible mess. Just when things were at their darkest, a ray of hope broke through.

Talk About It

- Both Adam and Eve refused to take responsibility for their actions, and tried to pin the blame on someone else. Most of us have done that at some point, especially if we had no way of fixing the problem we had created. Think of a time when you did this. How were you feeling in that moment? Sad? Scared? Angry? Ashamed? Why do you think you felt that way?

- God sent Jesus to pay the price for our sins, but the Bible still says we are supposed to confess them. Why do you think it's important to own up to our bad behavior?

Stomping on Serpents: The Kingdom Strikes Back!

And I will put enmity between you and the woman, and between your offspring and hers; he will crush your head, and you will strike his heel (Genesis 3:15).

It's important to understand that the curse is not what God wants for creation, for man and woman. Over the centuries, the first three chapters of Genesis have been used as an excuse for many horrible things, from environmental exploitation and cruelty to animals, from wars and torture to the mistreatment and oppression of women. But make no mistake—those things are a result of human sin, and go against God's will. Romans 8 tells us that Jesus came to undo the curse, to break the power of sin and death over humanity and the world.

Genesis 3:15 is what theologians call the *protoeuangelion*, which means "first good news." Right when everything had fallen apart, God promised to send an "offspring," born of a woman, who will destroy the serpent and all the mischief he has caused. It's the first time the Bible mentions God's plan to set things right by sending Jesus!

But here's the cool thing. The Hebrew word used for "offspring," *zar*, is both singular and plural. Jesus dealt Satan his death blow, but as fellow "offspring," brothers and sisters in Christ, we're invited to join the battle against sin and its death-dealing effects!

Even though we humans messed up, and continue to mess up, God has never given up on his original plan of using us to build his kingdom here on earth. Each and every one of us, male and female, young and old, are invited to throw ourselves into the battle for the planet—a battle that is already won, but hasn't quite wrapped up yet. The kingdom strikes back!

Talk About It

- Adam tried to blame Eve for the fall. Unfortunately, many generations have followed his example, and pointed to Genesis 3 as proof that men should "rule over" women—that men should be the leaders, and women should submit to them. Have you ever heard anyone talk like that? How would you respond to them? Are these ideas good ones? (encourage them to support their ideas with Scripture)

- What are some of the ways people you know are fighting back against the effects of the curse? Do you know a nurse who works with cancer patients, a farmer who produces crops that feed thousands of people, a counselor who helps couples heal their relationships, a missionary who encourages people to get in right relationship with God? What are some ways you can push back against sin's death-dealing effects?

Activity

Two Truths and a Lie

Sometimes, the most convincing lies are the ones that sound the most like the truth. Gather your group into a circle, and choose one person to be the first "truth-teller." The truth-teller needs to tell the group three things about themselves — two things that are true, and one thing that is a lie. Have people vote on which "truth" they think is a lie.

Did most people guess correctly? Once the truth-teller has revealed which truth was actually a lie, move on to the next person in the circle, and let them be the truth-teller. This game is a lot of fun, and a great way to get to know each other better while thinking about what makes a lie really convincing.

SESSION 3

— 3 —

The People of the Promise: Then and Now

Optional Bible Reading

Genesis 12

Primary Texts

The Lord had said to Abram, "Go from your country, your people and your father's household to the land I will show you. I will make you into a great nation, and I will bless you; I will make your name great, and you will be a blessing. I will bless those who bless you, and whoever curses you I will curse; and all peoples on earth will be blessed through you" (Genesis 12:1-3).

Understand, then, that those who have faith are children of Abraham....So in Christ Jesus you are all children of God through faith, for all of you who were baptized into Christ have clothed yourselves with Christ. There is neither Jew nor Gentile, neither slave nor free, nor is there male and female, for you are all one in Christ Jesus (Galatians 3:7, 26-28).

Blessed to Be a Blessing

Things got bad after Adam and Eve were banished from the garden. Really bad. The first several chapters of Genesis show humanity's downward spiral as the people of the world pulled further and further away from God, indulging themselves in violence, pride, and all kinds of evil.

In Genesis 12, God unveils a new strategy, a plan that will provide the structure, focus, and context for the rest of the Old Testament. In some ways, it's version 3.0 of the approach God started out with, with Adam and Eve: one man and one woman would multiply into a new people, a people who would show the world what it was like to live in a relationship with God, and carry the promise of the Savior mentioned in Genesis 3:16 in their DNA. These people were Abram and Sarai (later re-named Abraham and Sarah), a wealthy, elderly couple originally from the Mesopotamian metropolis of Ur.

Genesis 12:1-3 says:

> The Lord had said to Abram, "Go from your country, your people and your father's household to the land I will show you. I will make you into a great nation, and I will bless you; I will make your name great, and you will be a blessing. I will bless those who bless you, and whoever curses you I will curse; and all peoples on earth will be blessed through you."

Do you notice how similar these instructions are to the those God gave in Genesis 1?

Vv.	Genesis 1	Vv.	Genesis 12
28b	"fill the earth and subdue it.	1	"Go from your country, your people and your father's houshold to the land I will show you."
28a	"increase in number"	2	"I will make you into a great nation"
28a	God blessed them and said to them, "Be fruitful"	2, 3	"I will bless you...and all peoples on earth will be blessed through you."

Once again, God's followers are going to have to venture outside of their comfortable, familiar territory, extending their range of influence. Once again, they are going to multiply, this time into a great nation. Once again, this will happen to fulfill God's good purposes for his creation—to bless all the peoples of the earth.

Talk About It

1. All the people of the earth were blessed by Abraham and Sarah, because Jesus was their descendant. But can you think of other ways that Abraham and Sarah, or their descendants the Israelites, blessed the people around them? What about you? Does your relationship with God make you a blessing to others, whether they know God or not? How?

2. Abraham and Sarah also made a lot of mistakes in their relationships with the people they came in contact with, and with one another. Usually, this was because they lacked faith—because they were insecure or afraid, and relied on their own solutions, instead of God's. Have you ever hurt somebody, physically or emotionally, to compensate for your own insecurity? Has somebody hurt you out of their insecurity? How might things be different if we trusted God to look out for our best interests, instead of insisting on handling things ourselves?

The People of the Promise, Then

From Genesis 12 on, the Old Testament basically tells the story of Abraham and Sarah's descendants, the Hebrew people—their history, their laws, their poetry, their wisdom, their mistakes, their tragedies, and their triumphs. 2,000-plus years of Hebrew history are written out for our examination.

The great thing about this is that we can see how God's people dealt with all sorts of different situations—what they did right, what they did wrong, and how their stories turned out in the end. And even though these events took place in the ancient world, people haven't changed much in the last several thousand years. We deal with the same issues, in modern disguises.

Don't get along with your siblings? Check out the stories of Cain and Abel (Genesis 4:1-16), Jacob and Esau (Genesis 27), Absalom and Amnon (Genesis 13). Maybe your brother isn't so bad after all, huh?

Feel up against the odds joining a team or pursuing a profession where you would be in the minority? Read up on Deborah (Judges 4, 5), who led Israel boldly in a time when women were treated like property. She refused to let bullies intimidate her or her people.

Perhaps you have a parent who struggles with mental illness, or makes destructive decisions? Jonathan could commiserate. Even though his father, King Saul (1 Samuel 13-31), became mentally unstable and caused all sorts of trouble, Jonathan conducted himself admirably.

Think you could never turn your life around after some of the things you've done? Read about Rahab (Joshua 2:1-6:25), a Canaanite prostitute who threw herself at God's mercy and wound up becoming one of Jesus' ancestors!

The stories go on and on: the stuttering shepherd terrified of God's call to speak (Moses, Exodus 4:10-11), the widowed immigrant working hard to support her family (Ruth), the brainy diplomat living out his faith in a hostile environment (Daniel), the compliant queen who took a stand when her husband's orders threatened her people (Esther). The Old Testament is a goldmine of wisdom on how to live—and how not to live—your life in a way the honors God and blesses others.

Talk About It

- The Old Testament is full of different kinds of literature: historical narratives (stories), poetry, laws, prophesies, and wisdom literature (like Proverbs). Why do you think God included all these different types of writing, instead of sticking with simpler instructions on how to be a faithful follower of God?

- Some people don't spend much time studying the Old Testament, especially the laws given to the Israelites, because they don't think it's relevant to their life or their walk with God. What do you think? What can you learn from the laws and fulfilled prophesies God gave to ancient people?

The People of the Promise, Now

Throughout the Old Testament, God patiently taught the Israelites, using the words of the law and the prophets to instruct them on how to live justly, love mercy, and walk humbly with God in whatever circumstances they found themselves. While God was still at work in the lives of people outside Israel, Israel was given a special role to play in bringing their world to God, demonstrating what it was like to live in relationship with their Creator.

The same is true of Christians nowadays. As followers of Jesus, we are called first of all to know him, and then to go out and share him with others! As we walk with Jesus and learn from him, our lives should serve as an example of what it is like to live in relationship with God, and should bless those around us.

Talk About It

- In Galatians 3:7, 28-29, the apostle Paul draws the connection between the Israelites and the Christians. "Understand, then, that those who have faith are children of Abraham....There is neither Jew nor Gentile, neither slave nor free, nor is there male and female, for you are all one in Christ Jesus. If you belong to Christ, then you are Abraham's seed, and heirs according to the promise." What are we heirs of? And what is this promise Paul is talking about? There are several different ways you could answer this question, so don't be afraid to share your thoughts and ideas.

- What are some ways that you can learn more about God and grow in your relationship with Jesus? Get creative and share your ideas!

Activity

Bible Charades

The leader will have to tailor this game to the group's Bible knowledge. Break the group into two teams, and have one person from each team come up for each round, for a total of two actors. Whisper a well-known Old Testament story (using Bible stories about both men and women, such as Esther, David and Goliath, Ruth and Boaz, Moses, or Deborah) into their ears, explaining a bit about the story if necessary. Then set a timer for two to three minutes, and have them act out the story.

Let one team call out all their guesses about what story is being acted out, while the other stays silent. If they guess correctly before the time runs out, their team gets a point. If they don't, the other team gets one chance to guess what the story was. If neither team guesses correctly, the leader should give the answer.

Call up two new actors for the next round, and let the other group call out their guesses, while the first group remains silent. Keep going for as long as you like!

SESSION 4

— 4 —

The Unconventional King(dom)

Optional Bible Reading

Luke 1 and 2

Primary Texts

The Spirit of the Lord is on me, because he has anointed me to proclaim good news to the poor. He has sent me to proclaim freedom for the prisoners and recovery of sight for the blind, to set the oppressed free, to proclaim the year of the Lord's favor (Luke 4:18-19).

If anyone comes to me and does not hate father and mother, wife and children, brothers and sisters — yes, even their own life — such a person cannot be my disciple. And whoever does not carry their cross and follow me cannot be my disciple (Luke 14:26-27).

Therefore go and make disciples of all nations (Matthew 28:19).

An Unconventional Strategy

If you were about to launch a high-stakes plan to save the world from the worst evil humanity has ever known, who would you tell first? Who would you pursue as your first recruit? Would you chose the president, prime minister, or secretary of the United Nations? A small team of Navy SEALS, or the world's foremost military genius? Would you recruit scientists who could create advanced weapons, gifted speakers who could inspire people to action, rally the armies of the earth around your cause?

Not God. When God launched his counteroffensive against the prince of this world, the first person he told and invited to take part was a young teenage girl named Mary from an oppressed people group.

Typical.

And that was only the beginning of Jesus' counter-intuitive life and ministry. The Israelites had waited thousands of years for the messiah God promised them, but when he showed up, he was nothing like what they had expected. The Israelites expected a powerful king. Jesus was a humble carpenter-turned-rabbi. The Israelites wanted a dignified political leader. Jesus refused political power, and spent time with people his society scorned: women and children, tax collectors and prostitutes, Samaritans, sinners, and people with diseases and disabilities. The Israelites wanted someone to rescue them from the Romans. Jesus wanted to rescue them from themselves, and the power sin held over their lives.

Talk About It

- Mary was probably in her early teens when God called her to undertake one of the most important tasks in human history: to be the mother of the messiah. It was a difficult and dangerous assignment, and Mary took it on knowing that it would involve pain, rejection, and humiliation. Joseph, her husband-to-be, could even have demanded her execution! Does it surprise you that God would use someone about your age for such an important purpose? Does it change your perception of what you might be capable of contributing to God's kingdom? How?

The Unconventional King(dom)

Because we have the Bible, and live in a society that has been influenced by its teachings, it's hard for us to comprehend how counter-cultural Jesus' actions were in his day. Oh, the principles had been carried over from the Old Testament. In fact, in Luke 4:18-19, Jesus read from the scroll of Isaiah to describe what his ministry would be like:

> The Spirit of the Lord is on me, because he has anointed me to proclaim good news to the poor. He has sent me to proclaim freedom for the prisoners and recovery of sight for the blind, to set the oppressed free, to proclaim the year of the Lord's favor.

But no one had managed to live out the principles set forth in the Old Testament — principles of justice, compassion, and faithfulness to God — like Jesus did.

So, what was so radical about Jesus' life? Here are just a few examples:

In Jesus' day, women weren't educated or allowed to study the scriptures. They relied on whatever they heard in the synagogues or from male relatives.

But Jesus invited women into his inner circle (in fact, a group of women traveled with Jesus and the twelve disciples, Luke 8:1-3). Jesus horrified his followers by discussing theology with a Samaritan divorcee (John 4:1-42). He also defended Mary of Bethany when she "sat at Jesus' feet" as his disciple — something women weren't allowed to do — instead of helping her sister Martha with the dinner preparations (Luke 10:38-42).

In Jesus' day, people assumed that people with long-term illnesses and disabilities were being punished for sin, and often avoided them (John 9:2).

But Jesus touched contagious lepers (Luke 5:12-13), healed women with taboo bleeding problems (Luke 8:43-48), and welcomed a steady stream of people with broken bodies, minds, and hearts — people most religious leaders would have ignored or turned away.

In Jesus' day, many people believed that the best way to follow God was to establish Israel as an independent nation, and fight off outsiders who didn't follow God's laws.

But Jesus taught people to love their enemies and pray for those who persecuted them (Matthew 5:44), and eventually he sent his disciples out beyond Israel's borders to tell those "outsiders" all about him (Acts).

Really, that's a good definition of the good news — that through Jesus' life, death, and resurrection, all of us "outsiders" (and we're all "outsiders") are invited to be "insiders," reconciled to God and to one another. The barriers that used to separate us don't apply in Jesus' kingdom.

Of course, it was Jesus' death and resurrection that set us free from the ultimate consequences of the curse of sin and death. But Jesus' life was important, too. It set the example, and showed us how we are supposed to live as followers of God in a fallen world.

Talk About It

- Many of the things Jesus said and did were shocking to the people of his day, especially the religious leaders. If Jesus was walking the earth nowadays, do you think he would still be shocking people? How?

- Jesus could have used his God-given power and authority for his own earthly benefit, but instead he humbled himself, and used his power to serve others. As followers of Jesus, we're called to do the same thing. How might you use the gifts, resources, and influence God has given you to serve others?

Following Jesus Out of Our Comfort Zone

In Matthew 28:16, Jesus tells his followers to "go out and make disciples of all nations." We use this verse a lot when we're talking about evangelism, but sometimes we forget how it applies to our own lives. Being a Christian isn't just about believing certain things, or following certain rules. Being a Christian is about being Jesus' disciple—walking with him, learning from him, and modeling your life after his.

Remember way back in Genesis 1, when God created human beings to bear God's image? Being a Christian means that you bear Jesus' image, and are called to act as his representative on earth.

There are many great benefits to following Jesus (not the least of which is eternal life), but being a disciple also comes with a steep cost, a cost Jesus himself urges potential followers to consider. In Luke 14:26-27, Jesus says,

> If anyone comes to me and does not hate father and mother, wife and children, brothers and sisters—yes, even their own life—such a person cannot be my disciple. And whoever does not carry their cross and follow me cannot be my disciple.

Now, that does not mean that we are supposed to literally hate the people we love, but it does mean that our commitment to Jesus needs to leave our commitment to everything else in the dust.

What if Mary had been more worried about her relationship with Joseph than she was about her relationship with God?

What if Jesus had been more interested in preserving his own life than securing our salvation on the cross?

What if your desire to _____ is stronger than your desire to follow Jesus?

Thankfully, Mary and Jesus took the hard road of discipleship, following God even when it was lonely, scary, and downright painful. What about you? Will you follow Jesus, or will you follow the path of your own desires?

Talk About It

- What, for you, is the hardest part of being a disciple of Jesus? What might you have to give up, or hold loosely, in order to follow Jesus more closely?

- What helps you stay on track when following Jesus gets hard? Do you talk with a trusted friend? Spend time worshipping God? Read your Bible? Take a long, quiet walk?

- None of us follow Jesus perfectly. We all mess up, make mistakes, and stumble in our walk with Jesus. When that happens, we need to ask for forgiveness, and let God put us back on track. If you'd like, share about a time that has happened in your life. How did you mess up, and how did God restore you?

Activity

Dancing Disciples

Being a disciple isn't just about believing what the teacher says. It's about doing what the teacher does! Have one "reviewer" leave the room, and choose one brave soul to be the "dance teacher." After the dance teacher demonstrates a dance move for the group to start off with (the sillier the better), have everyone scatter around the room, facing the center. Call the reviewer back in, turn on some tunes, and start dancing!

Explain to the reviewer that it is their job to figure out who is leading the dance. The dance teacher needs to change the moves every twenty seconds or so, and the rest of the group needs to follow along as quickly as possible. Once the reviewer finds the dance teacher, turn off the music and end the game, or choose a new reviewer and dance teacher!

SESSION 5

— 5 —

Wind and Fire: An Unstoppable Combination

Optional Bible Reading:

Acts 2

Primary Texts:

> But you will receive power when the Holy Spirit comes on you;
> and you will be my witnesses in Jerusalem, and in all Judea and
> Samaria, and to the ends of the earth (Acts 1:8).

Ripe for the Harvest

Imagine the scene. Jerusalem was bursting at the seams, packed
with observant Jews from around the world celebrating Pentecost,
the festival of the first harvest of the year. Jesus had only recently
ascended into heaven, and 120 of his followers, men and women,
young and old, were crammed together in one place, praying. Jesus
had told them to go out into all the world, making disciples of all
nations. But he also told them to wait, to stay in Jerusalem until the

Holy Spirit came on them, giving them the power they needed to carry out this mind-boggling mission.

Suddenly, a sound like a hurricane hit the house, and holy fire appeared above each of their heads. Supernaturally emboldened and empowered, the believers poured out of their enclave and into the streets. Men and women, some probably no older than you, began preaching about Jesus to the crowds gathered in Jerusalem—and not just preaching, but preaching in the native languages of the listeners!

Some people insisted the preachers were drunk: unqualified rabble-rousers babbling heretical nonsense. But others listened, unable to ignore what God was doing through these startlingly ordinary women and men. It's tough to explain an uneducated fisherman who is suddenly fluent in Greek, or a Jewish mom preaching the house down in Parthian.

That Pentecost, the early church celebrated its first harvest, too—a harvest of about 3,000 new believers! Jesus had returned to heaven, but the Holy Spirit rushed into the void like wind and fire, enabling Jesus' followers to continue and expand his ministry. The good news was about to spread across the ancient world like wildfire, consuming dry traditions that kept people separated from God and one another, and making way for fresh growth.

Talk About It

- Has God ever done something that surprised you, or shook up your ideas about what following God looks like?

- Why do you suppose Jesus told his followers to wait? Have you ever had to wait to do something you knew you were supposed to do, but couldn't yet? Talk about it!

Available to Everyone

While Pentecost was definitely the beginning of something new, the Holy Spirit had been at work in people's lives long before then. In the Old Testament, the Holy Spirit revealed God's plans to people like Abraham (Genesis 15:1-5) and Rebekah (Genesis 25:21-23), gave instructions through leaders like Moses (Exodus 3:1-10) and Deborah (Judges 4:4-7), and spoke through prophets like Hosea (Hosea 1:1) and Huldah (2 Kings 22:14-20). In Psalm 51, David implores God not to take the Holy Spirit from him, even though he had sinned by committing adultery with Bathsheba and having her husband killed. The Holy Spirit is all over the first few chapters of Luke, filling people, coming on people, and sharing beautiful secrets.

So what changed at Pentecost?

The answer is that the kingdom had breached enemy lines and become a present spiritual reality for followers of Jesus.

Throughout the Old Testament, the prophets talked about a time when God would restore Israel, the messiah would rule the people justly, and everyone would enjoy a close, personal relationship with God. This long-awaited kingdom is what Peter was alluding to when he quoted the prophet Joel in Acts 2, to explain why his friends were babbling away in foreign languages.

> In the last days, God says, I will pour out my Spirit on all people. Your sons and daughters will prophesy, your young men will see visions, your old men will dream dreams. Even on my servants, both men and women, I will pour out my spirit in those days, and they will prophesy (Acts 2:17-18).

Jesus inaugurated this kingdom during his time on earth. It has not been fully realized, and won't be until he comes again, but the coming of the Holy Spirit at Pentecost is a taste of things to come. Everyone who pledges their allegiance to Jesus and becomes part of this new Kingdom has direct, 24/7 access to the wisdom and life-changing power of God through the Holy Spirit. No prophets, priests, or middle-men required.

Talk About It

- As followers of Christ, we have the Holy Spirit to guide us, but we need to take the time to seek God and listen for what the Holy Spirit has to say. What are some ways you could slow down and listen for the Holy Spirit this week? By reading the Bible? Through worship? In prayer?

Breaking Down Barriers to Build Up the Kingdom

If you had been among the crowd in Jerusalem on Pentecost, you might have been just as surprised by who was preaching as the fact that they were speaking in different languages. While there were occasional exceptions, the Jews were used to their religious leaders being carefully-educated men of a certain class. That Jesus' rag-tag band of fishermen, tax collectors, housewives, and ex-prostitutes were preaching with authority was astonishing enough. The fact that there were women among them preaching? Unheard of.

The Holy Spirit has a way of turning the world's power structures on their heads. When religion becomes a cultural institution, its leadership tends to look like the world's — the same sort of people, running things the same sort of way. But when the Holy Spirit is given free rein, things get shaken up.

The Holy Spirit does not discriminate based on age, gender, ethnicity, or social status, and neither should we. Gifts are given to be used for the good of the church, the body of Christ, and the advancement of God's kingdom. And God's kingdom tends to look different than the world's!

Talk About It

- The Holy Spirit does not discriminate based on age, gender, ethnicity, or social status. Do you? Do the people around you? If so, how could you bring about positive change? Talk about it!

Activity

Catching Fire

Choose one person to be the "fire fighter," and have them leave the room. Choose another person to be the "spark," then call the fire fighter back in. Seat everyone in a circle, with the fire fighter standing in the middle.

Explain that every time the spark winks at a person, that person will stand up. The group's objective is to get as many people standing as possible before the fire fighter guesses who the spark is. The fire fighter's objective is to find the spark with as few guesses as possible, preferably less than three. The game is no fun if the fire fighter just goes around the circle asking everyone if they are the spark!

A variation of this game is for people to start singing, or humming, or beating a rhythm on their knees after the spark winks at them. The building noise and chaos adds to the confusion, and the fun!

SESSION 6

— 6 —

Being the Body: Rocking your Role and Living in Love

Optional Bible Reading:

1 Corinthians 12

Primary Texts:

> There are different kinds of gifts, but the same Spirit distributes them. There are different kinds of service, but the same Lord. There are different kinds of working, but in all of them and in everyone it is the same God at work. Now to each one the manifestation of the Spirit is given for the common good (1 Corinthians 12:4-7).

> And let us consider how we may spur one another on toward love and good deeds, not giving up meeting together, as some are in the habit of doing, but encouraging one another — and all the more as you see the Day approaching (Hebrews 10:24-25).

Being the Body

So, we've learned that as followers of Christ, our mission is to multiply disciples who will reflect God's image to the world, and partner with God in building up God's kingdom on earth. We've looked at the stories, from Genesis to Acts, of how ordinary, everyday people followed God's calling on their lives—or not. And we've learned that the Holy Spirit empowers us to do the things God has planned for us, giving us everything we need to live holy lives and carry out God's will.

1 Corinthians 12 goes into even more detail about how God's good plans for the world will be accomplished through us. The Holy Spirit gives each of us spiritual gifts—gifts like teaching, healing, leading, giving, encouragement, and many other things—that we are supposed to use for the common good. And even though we each have our own unique gifts, they aren't meant to be used in isolation. Instead, we're supposed to work together to accomplish God's purposes.

1 Corinthians 12:18-20 says,

> But in fact God has placed the parts in the body, every one of them, just as he wanted them to be. If they were all one part, where would the body be? As it is, there are many parts, but one body.

It's important for each of us to discover what our spiritual gifts are, to grow in them and use them to the best of our God-given ability. But it's equally important to pay attention to the gifts God has given the people around us, to encourage them to develop their gifts and work with them to build up God's kingdom.

Talk About It

- Do you have any ideas about what your spiritual gifts might be? What are some ways you might develop and use those gifts?

- What gifts do you see in other people you know? What are some ways you could encourage them to use and develop their gifts?

"But Women Aren't Supposed to _____."

Some people think that women aren't supposed to use certain gifts in church—that only men can be pastors, deacons, elders, teachers, or leaders. This belief is based mainly on two Bible passages where the apostle Paul says women should learn silently in church, and not try to teach or boss the men around: 1 Timothy 2:11-12 and 1 Corinthians 14:33-35. The question we need to ask when these two verses appear is whether Paul meant women to always remain silent in church and never use gifts of speaking, teaching, or leading when men are around, or whether those instructions were addressing specific problems in specific situations.

In this case, it's pretty clear that Paul was addressing a specific problem (probably women who had never been allowed an education, and had a lot to learn before they could speak or teach without causing problems), because Paul praised women for teaching and leading in other passages. Paul bragged up his relative Junia (who was an apostle, a position that carried incredible authority, Romans 16:7), his friend Priscilla (who taught Apollos, one of the early church's most effective evangelists, Acts 18:18-26, Romans 16:3-4), the deacon Phoebe (who brought the book of Romans to Rome, and probably explained it to church leaders there, Romans 16:1-2), and a whole host of other women he describes as co-workers in ministry (Romans 16). Paul would be horrified to learn that people are using his words to keep women from using the gifts God gave them!

God doesn't give gifts according to gender, and the gifts God gives are meant to be used. It would be a sin to hide them away, like presents sitting unopened and unused on the back shelf of a closet, just because someone else thinks that particular gift might not be appropriate for you. If God has given you a gift, open it up and use it for the common good! Paul says to "fan into flame" the gift God gives you (2 Timothy 1:6).

Talk About It

- Has anyone ever told you that only men can do certain things in church? How did you feel about that? How do you think God feels about that?

- Have you ever hidden or denied the gifts God gave you, or tried to suppress someone else's gifts? Why? How can you avoid doing that in the future?

What's Love Got to do With It?

It's no coincidence that the Bible's most extensive passage about spiritual gifts is followed by its most famous chapter about love. As the apostle Paul said in 1 Corinthians 13:1-3,

> If I speak in the tongues of men or of angels, but do not have love, I am only a resounding gong or a clanging cymbal. If I have the gift of prophecy and can fathom all mysteries and all knowledge, and if I have a faith that can move mountains, but do not have love, I am nothing. If I give all I possess to the poor and give over my body to hardship that I may boast, but do not have love, I gain nothing.

Paul knew that it is easy to get so swept up in the adventure of using our gifts and doing good works that we lose sight of the relationships at the core of it all, and forget about the commandments to love God and one another. Volunteering at church won't make up for ignoring your relationship with God. It doesn't matter how well you know the Bible if you are impatient or unkind to the people you want to share Christ with. If you'll go house to house collecting canned goods for the food shelf, but won't sit next to a kid who can't afford the right kind of clothes in the lunchroom, your service project rings kind of hollow, doesn't it? We need to love one another!

Hebrews 10:24-25 says,

> And let us consider how we may spur one another on toward
> love and good deeds, not giving up meeting together, as some are
> in the habit of doing, but encouraging one another—and all the
> more as you see the Day approaching.

As the body of Christ, we need to be constantly encouraging one another:

- encouraging one another to discover, develop, and use our gifts

- encouraging one another to go out and make disciples, and expand
  God's kingdom by working for the common good

- encouraging one another not to lose sight of the most important
  things: our relationship with God, and our love for others.

As followers of Christ, we have been called out. Now let's go do
this thing!

Talk About It

- Where do you need encouragement right now? And how could
  you encourage others? Talk about it as a group, and commit to
  encouraging one another!

Activity

Building Blind

Break into groups of 4 or 5 people. Choose one person to be the
"architect" in each group, and divide building materials (blocks
or Legos, pretzels and marshmallows, cardboard tubes and tape,
or whatever is on hand) evenly between the remaining members.

Blindfold everyone but the architect, or simply have them close their eyes.

The blindfolded members have to work together to build a single structure out of the materials they have been given, following the architect's instructions. The architect can't touch the construction, and the builders can't peek, until all of the building materials have been used (and you have to use them all). What sorts of crazy constructions did the different groups come up with?

About the Authors

Aaron Armstrong has worked with youth for over fifteen years, in church, para-church, and music ministry settings. Passionate about teaching, encouragement, and evangelism, he studied music at the University of Wisconsin-Superior, and is a graduate of Youth for Christ's Summer Institute of Missions and Evangelism and Relational Youth Evangelism.

Jenny Rae Armstrong is an award-winning freelance writer who is passionate about encouraging people to pursue God's calling on their life. She majored in global studies at Northwestern College in St. Paul, MN, and is a graduate of Youth for Christ's Summer Institute of Missions and Evangelism and Relational Youth Evangelism.

Aaron and Jenny live in northern Wisconsin with their four sons.

About Christians for Biblical Equality

Christians for Biblical Equality (CBE) is a nonprofit organization of Christian men and women who believe that the Bible, properly interpreted, teaches the fundamental equality of men and women of all ethnic groups, all economic classes, and all age groups, based on the teachings of Scriptures such as Galatians 3:28:

> "There is neither Jew nor Gentile, neither slave nor free, nor is there male and female, for you are all one in Christ Jesus" (NIV 2011).

Mission Statement

CBE affirms and promotes the biblical truth that all believers — without regard to gender, ethnicity or class — must exercise their God-given gifts with equal authority and equal responsibility in church, home and world.

Core Values

We believe the Bible teaches...

- Believers are called to mutual submission, love and service.
- God distributes spiritual gifts without regard to gender, ethnicity or class.
- Believers must develop and exercise their God-given gifts in church, home and world.
- Believers have equal authority and equal responsibility to exercise their gifts without regard to gender, ethnicity or class and without the limits of culturally-defined roles.
- Restricting believers from exercising their gifts — on the basis of their gender, ethnicity or class — resists the work of the Spirit of God and is unjust.
- Believers must promote righteousness and oppose injustice in all its forms.

Opposing Injustice

CBE recognizes that injustice is an abuse of power, taking from others what God has given them: their dignity, their freedom, their resources, and even their very lives. CBE also recognizes that prohibiting individuals from exercising their God-given gifts to further his kingdom constitutes injustice in a form that impoverishes the body of Christ and its ministry in the world at large. CBE accepts the call to be part of God's mission in opposing injustice as required in Scriptures such as Micah 6:8.

Envisioned Future

Christians for Biblical Equality envisions a future where all believers are freed to exercise their gifts for God's glory and purposes, with the full support of their Christian communities.

Join the Movement

CBE members are extraordinary advocates for Christ's liberation from human limitations imposed by gender, ethnicity, or class. By joining CBE, you stand together with Christians around the world who promote the biblical truth of equality. As a member, you receive cutting-edge resources on what the Bible says about gender and justice. And your dues support and sustain our ministry!

Membership benefits include: a subscription to *Priscilla Papers*, our quarterly, award-winning academic journal; a subscription to *Mutuality*, our quarterly, award-winning popular magazine; 50% off CBE-produced recordings and 15%-20% off all other resources at our online bookstore; discounts on registration to CBE conferences; access to e-versions of recent issues of our journals; and more.

Visit cbeinternational.org/membership to join today!

www.ingramcontent.com/pod-product-compliance
Lightning Source LLC
Chambersburg PA
CBHW050949030426
42339CB00007B/351

* 9 7 8 1 9 3 9 9 7 1 0 1 2 *